The Journey Home

Marie Rose

BALBOA.PRESS

A DIVISION OF HAY HOUSE

Balboa Press books may be ordered through booksellers or by contacting:

Balboa Press
A Division of Hay House
1663 Liberty Drive
Bloomington, IN 47403
www.balboapress.co.uk
UK TFN: 0800 0148647 (Toll Free inside the UK)
UK Local: 02036 956325 (+44 20 3695 6325 from outside the UK)

Because of the dynamic nature of the Internet, any web addresses or
links contained in this book may have changed since publication and
may no longer be valid. The views expressed in this work are solely those
of the author and do not necessarily reflect the views of the publisher,
and the publisher hereby disclaims any responsibility for them.

The author of this book does not dispense medical advice or prescribe
the use of any technique as a form of treatment for physical, emotional,
or medical problems without the advice of a physician, either directly
or indirectly. The intent of the author is only to offer information
of a general nature to help you in your quest for emotional and
spiritual well-being. In the event you use any of the information in
this book for yourself, which is your constitutional right, the author
and the publisher assume no responsibility for your actions.

Any people depicted in stock imagery provided by Getty Images are
models, and such images are being used for illustrative purposes only.
Certain stock imagery © Getty Images.

Print information available on the last page.

ISBN: 978-1-9822-8145-8 (sc)
ISBN: 978-1-9822-8146-5 (e)

Balboa Press rev. date: 06/23/2020

To

Tamseeth

May your Dreams

come

True

Marie Rose

x

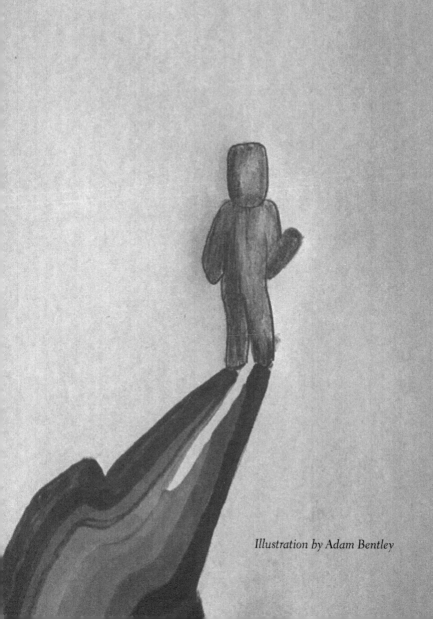

Illustration by Adam Bentley

True Colours

DREAM on through the memories of yesteryear .. go beyond and listen with your inner ear ..my dear

..away from fear and distraction ..your a fraction of the whole ..and also the whole ..like a drop in the ocean but also the ocean ..visions of the true will appear for you when your at ease ..inwards you will go to go with the eternal flow dreaming anew ..its up to you ..the world is your canvas ..paint your colours onto the screen ..pink and gold ..love will unfold for you when your true colours will shine through ..you can be seen for who you truly are ..remember your a star made from stardust and to return to star maker creator ..

Riding the Storm

RIDING the waves through the storm ..we tell ourselves it wont be long ..until we are in pastures new a world of true ...where we belong ...where lies have died and we are reborn ..with visions anew and oh so true from the heart of the matter ..connect to mother earth ..feel the beat under your feet ..this is your home frequency she will connect and nourish you to feel good ..we will begin to see more clearly love more dearly with 2020 vision it starts here this is our year ..with golden dreams in our hearts ..we will never walk alone when love rules the world and golden dreams begin to come true for me and for you and the entire human race ..happiness all over the place ..grace land .we can see clearly

now.. the storms will come and go ..but we know the sun will rise again and again ..so ride the rainbow of your dream choose the colours to create your part..in wonderment to come creating as you go from season to season be at one with nature feeling the sounds of birds and bees ..the rustling of leaves..feel the breeze blow away the cobwebs off your mind remember your one of a kind ..choose the vibes that you prefer ..and do please take care to choose wisely from your heart ..and soon you will be playing your part in authenticity ..a real fine place ..choose to be authentic and real ..clench the deal ..to remember to feel ..whats really real ..

Garden of Peace

IM in the garden of no name ..I really don't feel any pain..my life will never be the same again ..no labels ..no tags ..no t.v. Im feeling really free ..to be me ..free spirited with dreams and wishes coming through in visions I see in dreams I play with a different reality ..its beautiful and calm ..and no one can cause no harm to another here as love is all there is ..I believe we can choose to walk through this door ..with faith hope and charity ..begin at home in your heart ..walk on through what else can you do ..the porthole of your heart will call you ..dive in deeper than you'v been before ..go on to explore from the head to the heart ..its time to journey home within ..get out of the spin .that you've been in ..you'll soon be home once more ..with love to adore ..amore

Promised Land

TAKE my hand ..and on we will go shining our light throughout the day throughout the night keeping it lighthearted ..as we go into the natural flow ..no more intense ..melt down the defence ..you had around your heart ..start to feel the barriers come down one by one ..love has won ..and will come through ..you are made from love from above and below ..heavenly sent ..on a mission ..to bring heaven to earth ..connect mind heart and soul don't you know your true passion .. inside ..your natural beat ..can you feel the heat of passion anew coming up from the earth as she unites with us ..like a diamond in the rough you will shine and cut through the mud ..its in your blood ..to make the

change and the ancestors will take your hand to the promised land ..new earth is here ..lend me your inner ear ..and you will hear the whispering winds of change coming through straight to you ..

A S we start to enter the flow onwards and upwards we will go ..along our chosen path ..breaking free from the shadows of fear.. with each breaking dawn we will soon be home ..homeward bound ..feeling found.. as love calls us home to be a part of loving what is to witness what was ..to break free ..from pain ..it was only a game of right and wrong ..left and right .meet me in a field where there is no right or wrong no judge ..from above or below ..surrender to the warm and tenter love ...love is here..now..just flow ..from within ..enter beingness just observe ..released from emotional charge ..set yourself free to be ..your whole self ..shiny and new without the baggage you will get through

the gates of heaven ..open for you ..no more intense ..we've let down the fence of defence that was around your heart ..go on in now you have a very good part to play in this beautiful movie remember to play ..innocence will take you back to zero ..wipe the slate clean .. its all a dream ..start to co-create ..its never too late ..to open this gate heaven will wait ..

Be Here Now

BE present now .. enter into the power of now where you will feel at ease ..if you please ..where there is no disease ..here we are in the art of allowing ..what will be will be .. permission to be free.. practice this magical way of beingness each and every day ..released from the past ..unafraid of the future ..just being here now ..accept where your at ..get to the core ..and love will dissolve all the fear that was before ..go within ..dive deeper than before ..eventually you will find that your one of a kind ..unique ..and the gift that you are wont feel too far out of your reality ..so reach inside feel whats reel ..the treasure inside can no longer hide ..it was there all along .. what took you so long ..activated by being present ..that

in itself is a glorious gift ..to the world and to you ..so claim your presence by being present ..forgive to forget what was before ..you opened this door of perception anew ..its all up to you..forget the past ..go on and have a blast into the now future ..and your energy will rocket into the power of now here ..

Flow Dreaming

HIGH vibrations coming through to reach you and attune you ..to match the frequency of your hearts desire . . and ignite the passion.. in your soul ..open up ..come out of your cave ..relight your fire ..remember your dream awake ..its never too late ..flow dream all the way ..each and every day .open up to the new wave ..to carry us through the troubled waters of yesteryear.. we leave the past behind ..cross the bridge over troubled waters ..to crystal clear insight ..take time and space to see more clearly than you've ever seen before as your vision expands ..you will see beyond the limited view before you blew away the cobwebs of your mind and realised your one of a kind ..unique and beautiful

in your own way ..stay fresh with yourself and feel anew ..its all written in the new script awaiting you ..excitement and bubbles of joy will come up for you as you enter inside ..with a clear mind ..happy thoughts come through to make you smile .. Its been a while since you felt totally you ..your whole self all back together again ..anew ..reconditioned.. rewired.. upgraded to work especially for you..your wish is your command..the genie is out the bottle ..ask and it will be given ..don't be shy ..wave the past goodbye.. dreams can come true when you believe in you ..

Epiphany

A S you receive an epiphany ..time can stand still ..for a few seconds to see a new door to enter..a different stroke to paint onto your canvas..a new door to explore ..what are you waiting for ..its been there all along ..just waiting to activate you along your path of least resistance ..with a new song in your heart ..you can sing a mantra or a prayer ..do take care as you enter pastures new ..what will you do ..just be true ..and trust its a must..enter authenticity ..its a real fine place filled with grace..softer and sweet its such a treat..you'll want to tap your feet ..to the beat of your very own heart ..its where its at ..home at last in your home frequency ..your unique and not a freak ..to be different ..so bless you through

and through ..fear has left you ..close the
door behind you.. ..open to true and you
wont feel so blue ..let the waves of bliss
take you to the shore ..rest awhile ..and
your sure to smile in this heavenly
state ..vibrating through you ..enjoy ..and
be sure to return ..stay as long as you
wish ..paradise ..and bliss..we will always
be here ..

Beaming Bright

LIGHT heart skip through the dark ..no more intense we've let down the fence.. only love can see you through ..let love see through your eyes to project from your lens ..without the defence..enter through your heart porthole of true ..take a peek through rose tinted glasses if you will ..just to see what love can be seen ..wipe the world clean ..forgiving what was before ..you had your foot in the door of the heart path ..lit up for you to walk along ..you will never walk alone ..you will find a song in there to help you along ..what treasure you will find inside your chest when you get there ..to open more ..than ever before ..each day comes new ways to see your way home on your heart path ..so

let the fence melt down each one you come across..burning love will melt them for you ..go along now the path of least resistance..and wear your crown instead of a frown ..creator of your creation ..carry on with your inspiration ..as you go deeper and deeper you'll enter the flow and find yourself your piece of peace..a place of tranquil restoration ..day dream from here a while ..soon you will find a smile come over you ..paint your picture pink and gold ..red yellow and blue ..whatever feels good for you ..a new story will unfold ..as you go on and be so bold as to do what you've never been told ..step outside what you've been taught ..your out of your egotic mind ..mind how you go ..within the flow ..waves of creativity ....

its your time and space to create with all your might ..please keep the vibrations light and bright ..for others too ..feel the delight ..as you give ..then open to receive .forgive to forget ..from the power of your light heart ..a lighthouse in the dark and gloomy storms when ships go astray ..show them the way with your light beaming bright ..

ETERNAL spirit the gift of life is flowing through you ..each and every day ..what you create with this is up to you ..allow your spirit to take part ..and you will take flight out of the fright than you might have got caught up in ..caught in a trap ..theres no turning back ..let the past go ....take a leap of faith and allow this grace to come over you ..express your natural self ..your essence ..your natural gifts.. as nature intended ..express your whole self ..put your whole self into what you do and be true to you ..your spirit will inspire you to guide you through ..the rough and tumble ..to the diamond you ..your core self ..born again every day ..with abundance ..fresh and excited for what

lies ahead ..you will be lead ..in your journey through this matter ..this earth plane ..relate in her ship ..every thing is a relationship ..to relate ..she will help you through in all that you do ..its happening for all weather your big or small..each of us can open our heart more ..forgive to forget ..the key to set you free.. letting go of the seat of pain ..tears for fears ..so deep they could not weep ..for fear of drowning here .lost in sorrow ..unable to believe in a new tomorrow ..its been so long frozen in fear ..your heart can now melt my dear ..love is near ..

here to stay ..and will never go away ..again welcome back home in your heart ..heaven will wait ..always ..and forever eternal ..

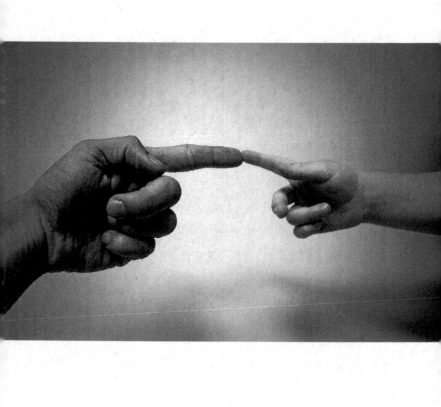

Connected

C ONNECTED to the divine plan..having gone through enough in the limited view.. from the fragmented self..reaching for more equilibrium ..balance and true..a new script will be given ..from the creator for you ..to see you through ..in the next chapter in life ..so close the door behind ..and make up your mind ..to go forward from here ..please lend me your ear to hear ..whispers gentle on your mind..forever more true..as troubles melt away like lemon drops ..walk on by ..over the bridge of troubles waters ..love will lay down ..and create a unique path for you ..so onward bound with your new scrip ..new ways ..new path ..sprinkled with beams of love ..joy and excitement ..you'll

be walking back to happiness ..waves are coming through the magnetic hue ..to connect you to mother earth..glistening golden dreams await to activate you ..to be true love ..theres enough for all ..fill up on the feeling of abundance ..self love ..self worth ..full steam ahead ..your on the love train ..of thought ..remember to take a deep breath ..take it all in ..rip up the old script ..you will be shown as you go ..into the flow ..the movie of your life ..no need to act ..and thats a fact ..as your authentic and real ..and done the deal ..crossed over.. the bridge ..pasters new ..quantum field of dreams ..dream on ..find your song ..we all have a song to sing..your heart will want to sing with the harmonious vibrations coming up for you ..

Peace

ULTIMATELY we all want peace ..the way to peace .. meditate ..its within ..you ..your true nature ..can hush the monkey mind ..calm your own inner storm ..connect to nature when you can ..the trees ..the plants ..flowers.. and bees ..so please make a connection and go within ..the inner realms will start to work with you ..to find balance ..calm the waters of your storm ..peace of mind ..as you go into the inner dimensions you will feel the depth of more ..theres more of you than meets the eye ..its all within for you to explore ..you will get a new sense ..perhaps a sixth sense will activate ..we all have this..this inner knowing ..intuition ..inner teacher..gut brain ..feeling for you what is true ..feeling and sensing for you ..so

trust ..a little bit more each day ..take your inner journey to tranquil peace..oh we are saying ..give peace a chance ..its a new pathway for you ..peaceful beingness.. no less ..too much thinking is out of date ..enter a new gate to beingness..with new earth harmonics its time to play in this vibrational universe ..so release the old way..its a new day ..to feel deeper into your universe ..one verse at a time ..will take you to where still waters run deep ..its so calm you could almost sleep ..so listen to the sound of golden silence now and then ..and enter your one of a kindness..love will grow ..within your flow ..to you anew ..a dewdrop from the ocean of love ..but also the ocean ..expansion happens when your at ease ..peace be with you ..

ITS now or never ..hold on tight as
the beings of light help you to release
all the fright ..break down ..break
through the old records that were playing
in your head ..its time to put them to
bed ..if you please ..the old stories that
you told yourself were true ..before you
knew ..there is a way back ..way back to
innocence ..back to the future ..bringing
your innocence into the here and now ..the
future looks bright ahead ..always be true
to a heart thats true ..your own heart
can communicate through you ..trust
in love ..its a must ..speak from your
heart ..with love on your side you wont
have to hide ..how you really feel ..now is
the time to speak your truth ..you have a
voice ..it can be heard ..to make a difference

in this world ..the world is a stage and each of us has a part to play ..each and every day ..reach out and touch someones hand ..help them across to the promised land ..if you can..what is there to leave behind but your essence ..your love ..your perfume ..your guidance ..your kindness.. leave the game of thrones ..theres no place for you there ..no need for greed or hunger ..no religion too ..Imagine your way out of that movie ..and do it your way ..you have a new script awaiting ..authentic and real co-creating from grace ..love ..bliss and joy ..high vibrations all around when you tune in ..turn on ..switch on your receptors to receive ..your new story ..leave behind the gory ..relax here in the glory ..for a while ..smile ..you have

the key inside to reset ..reactivate ..open up to the magic that you are ..love your vehicle of expression ..your body ..your somebody special ..we all are ..when we awaken in the dream ..out of the tragic ..drama -trauma ..star ignite ..full of light keep shining ..your a diamond ..a treasure ..all inside ..to find ..go in be bold ..a new story will unfold ..

The Windows of Your Soul

L OOKING through the windows of your eyes can you see your paradise ..you can if you look again deeper ..there will always be a trace of a heavenly trail to see ..to help you break free ..from monotony ..so take a peek again once more ..to explore ..and you could enter a new door ..like alice in wonderland ..theres a whole new world waiting to explore ..when you open a new door ..perception anew ..what am I to do ..enter ..to the world of enchantment ..delight and wonder ..like a child ..imagination plays a big part ..so get out of the race to where.. go within ..to no where ..now here ..image making ..projecting from your lens ..it makes no sense ..your mind will say ..but please take time to play ..with creative energy

coming through for you ..to see a different stroke to project onto your landscape ..take time to see more clearly now the rain has gone ..you will see the barriers that were in your way melt away ..the veils lifted ..in to me see ..intimacy..get intimate with the original creator as you were in the beginning ..you are the creator who put them there ..you can wipe the slate clean and start again ..reborn ..reawakened ..to your creative power ..within ..imagine ..what you can do ..to make this world a better place ..we can all participate ..its never too late ..all you have admired in another is in you too ..they are a mirror reflection just like you ..image making as you go ..theres so much more to you than meets the eye ..bye bye limited way ..I can see more than ever before 2020 vision ..is here ..my dear ..

Gene Genie

T HE law of attraction will work for you ..when your vibration is true ..with you whole self ..activated with passion for what you do ..and want to do ..so strong ..knowing it wont be long now ..as you've let go of the old story ..the story you came through ..from the ancestors ..the genes that carried you through ..now its up to you ..epigenetics ..we rise above and beyond ..the old melts away ..we came to create the new story ..this world will have her glory ..glorious and returned to her natural state ..paradise..heavenly bliss.. out of the old reptilian way ..we have evolved ..new earth ..new template ..the golden age is here ..have no fear ..high frequency vibes ..can you feel the good

vibrations ..tune in ..your genie is out
of the bottle ..your avatar..is here my
dear ..your star..make your wish upon your
star ..your wish is your command ..wish for
something grand ..and we will hold your
hand ..you could ask for more love ..bliss
and joy ..but do remember to come from
your heart ..when you take part ..in your
inner dreams and wishes ..as in the unified
field of dreams ..there is no fear ..my
dear ..unconditional love reigns here.. all
the way through in all that you do ..take
love with you ..

Rescue Me

PLEASE come and rescue me ..Ive been caught in a trance instead of a dance ..of authenticity ..synchronicity..caught in a trap ..as I always used to look back ..to where I was ..thinking too much about what I thought I had lost ..feelings of lack ..not in believe that the universe has my back .. don't look back in anger ..to point a finger of whose to blame for my pain..letting go of what was the muddy waters of yesterday ..negative emotions ..I want to release the memories..so I forgive to forget ..and realise ..with real eyes ..looking through with love .. a brighter story to unfold ..now ..I feel ready to come out of the cold ..and feel myself a bit bold ..not doing what I was told ..but thinking that I created

a sin ..lets throw that story in the bin ...to go where Ive never been before ..looking forward ..more and more ..knowing Ive been rescued ..picked up off the floor ..thank you so very much ..Im forevermore touched by my angel ..whose there ..whenever Im in despair ..picked up ..brushed off ..sprinkled with gold dust ..theres a new story waiting in the wings ..Im on the stage with my new part to play ..each and every day ..my angel is here ..whispering in my ear..with passion anew Im feeling the flame of this new desire ..relight my fire ..burning love ..hug me some more ..I do adore ..this feeling inside ..I cannot deny ..Im so grateful for my part in this new earth ..hallelujah..I was never really alone ..Im home once more ..

D O you know who you are really..your whole self ..in the movie ..just be totally real ..how you feel ..you can heal ..any pain ..its not a game ..or a race ..take your self to a place of grace within ..you can win your own love back ..to you ..out of the dark blue ..negative emotions can go ..with hoponopono .back to innocence .forgive to forget ...no matter where you have been you can wipe the slate clean ..end the struggle of doom and gloom ..its time for us to bloom and grow ..within the stream.. the river of life ..love ..your natural state ..of beingness..linger there a while..the air so fresh and sweet ..smell the fragrance here lifting your senses ..taste the sense of upliftment ..and soon you will melt ..soften

your mind ..do be kind ..enter the flow in order to grow .. ..the vortex..expand your vision ..expand your consciousness ..to see a whole new tomorrow the new dawn ..age of aquarius..when the moon is in the seventh house and jupiter aligns with mars ..then peace will guide the planets ..and love will steer the stars ..golden age is upon us ..let the sunshine in ..golden living ..dare to dream ..you are the dreamer of your reality ..wakey wakey rise and shine ..enter the divine ..dive in ....microcosmic..to macrocosmic.. golden rays streaming to you ..harmonic waves all over the place ..catch the waves ..open your mind ..your one of a kind ..one verse ..universe ..at a time ..your the creator of your dream ..dream a little

brighter ..a little more each day ..remember to play ..in your imagination ..a nation of magic ..this symphony all around ..in nature will be found ..listen to the sounds of nature ..be at one ..here ..your very near ..heaven will wait ..the gate is ajar ..open it a bit more ..its all waiting for you ..heartwarming ..welcome ..step inside love ..love who you are .. you are love..indeed..the seed was always there ..

Love Boat

IM in the boat ..feeling alone ..trying to keep afloat ..in all that I do ..I just want to be true ..to my heart and soul ..as I sail my ship down the river of life ..as I turn a corner round a bend in this journey ..I realise that I was never really alone ..love was always guiding me home ..having let go of the baggage of how it should be ..the expectancy..from old stories ..told before ..Im reaching for new horizons to explore ..new thought forms come to me to help me see ..more clearly ..where we are going ..me myself and I ..we cannot lie ..as we want to be true ..as the truth sets you free ..sounds fantastic to me ..freedom ..so rare ..I do want my share ..so I will practise being true to my very own heart ..to be a part of something

bigger ..the bigger picture so to speak ..im done with being too meek ..please can I have a peek ..at the dreams of tomorrow without so much sorrow..im glad to say ..ive been granted my wish ..to see crystal clear visions ..of this new earth wish..so much bliss..paradise is real..I wish you could feel this for you too ..Imagine below is only heaven ..above us only sky ..all the songs that make us feel again real ..will open us up to take us through ..the journey ..your favourite song will have a message for you..too..find your natural self..no sabotage ..no fear ..here ..harmonious vibes to keep you more alive ..will kick in ..get you out of the spin ..into the dream ..out of the scream ..one love one heart ..beat ..together ..in harmony ..each

has a part to play ..find your song ..to sing along ..your journey home ..in your ship.. relate to you too..be true ..life is what you make it ..love what is ..find your recipe ..for love ..its inside you ..a good place to start ..accept your amazing ..grace will follow..follow me follow you..lets be true to love ...and love will surely find us ..the power of love ..is all we need ..love is all you need ..

Remembrance

TAKE time to remember ..who you are ..where you came from ..from here to eternity ..we will go ..with momentum of who ..why ..and where..the big question may arise ..and give you a surprise..that if you go into yourself deeper and deeper ..you will find the keeper ..with the key inside ..your very soul ..yes it can be deep ..for some to peek ..they may not want to know..in fear of what they might find..but all that awaits is the treasure inside ..like a treasure chest way down at the bottom of the ocean ..you will get there in waves..when you get the notion ..to dive in deeper ..than you've ever been..now come clean ..its a beautiful treasure in your soul ..connected to the whole..all you've ever been..the treasure is your essence..

the gems that you accumulated..over each lifetime..richness of experience ..to enrich the soul..to make you more whole and complete..its very neat..and the wisdom is yours to keep..so remember to take a peek inside ..come out of your cave..dive in to the subconscious mind..clear out the weeds ..and the debris of programmes in the way ..your clear pathway will open for you ..with whispers..from your soul..a part of you that is whole ..grounded..with wisdom..to guide you through in all that you do..so take time to remember..become a member of your soul tribe..tribal by nature ..you want to belong ..thats why it can take so long ..if you have forgotten where you came from..due to amnesia.. lost on the surface mind ..anxious ..and

frayed ..the old records have been over played..so remember ..your a beautiful soul ..come to this planet for a reason ..and a season in the sun..let the sun shine in.. from here to infinity and beyond ..so flow with grace to this human place ..to reignite your light and wisdom..of your soul..bring this through your being..the art of allowing your essence to express ..your original blueprint..originality ..to express freely..deeply ..still waters run deep ..be still ..at ease..if you please ..

Awakening

INTO the realms of awakened souls ..onwards and upwards we go ..as we walk this new path ..being true.. step by step ..with conscious intent ..awake to assist in the paradigm shift ..going on ..change is inevitable..and we do have a choice..united we stand ..divided we fall..lets find a common thread ..to be led to pastures new ..the quantum field ..of infinite possibilities ..as creators ..we can dream ourselves awake in this dream ..take yourselves out of the box of limitation ..its a brand new nation ..end of the game of duality..right and wrong ..who s to blame

for your pain .. for how you feel ..lets do the deal and love for real ..unconditional rays of love ..coming in from above and below..the deep blue sea ..oh cant you see.. the connection to this beautiful planet.. gaia..her spirit is forever nurturing as we learn to bloom and grow ..like her flowers we are flowering too ..as we open our chakras ..like the lotus flowers..express our entire self ..whole self ..no longer fragmented piece of the whole but your whole multidimensional self ..all you've ever wanted to be from your true self .who you really are ..made from .star ..dust . ..star light..all is here ..keep it bright ..your inner light ignite ..take flight ..flying without wings..at the speed of sound..and vision ..

its very neat and such a treat to feel this whole and complete ..for now in the power of now ..day by day ..a new script will play out ..namaste

Starlight Express

A METEORITE of stars coming into earths orbit..from another galaxy..to help us reconnect..with our light ..the light inside that might have almost gone ..to a pilot light ..as we might have been on auto pilot ..struggling along our path..lost and feeling abandoned ..never fear ..love and light is here ..and now.. lets turn up the spark of divinity that you are.. the power that you are is within ..tap in..tune in..switch on..to who you really are ..starlight..turn up the volume ..speak your truth ..with compassion..fire..in your belly..ignite the passion..your gifts are your passion..the essence of your whole self.. from the community of one ..one love one heart..love for all your components.. each and every cell open to the love and

light ..come out of the fright..you will feel so vital and alive..bathed in the love and notion of a new tomorrow ..instead of drowning in emotion ..trust its a must.. your ship might rock and roll and you might feel a little shook up ..but this is good vibrations ..coming through strong to assist you move along your new path ..be brave..heart ..assisted with unconditional love..your fuel ..get fired up .. starlight.. ignite your sparks...lighten up ..out of the dense ..heavy ..baggage from the past ..let it all go ...you wont know yourself..you will feel brand new..loving you ..the greatest gift ..to be true ..love..

Liberty

AS we enter the flow ..onwards we go with perception anew..a way of being merging through us..the spirit within wants to dance the dance of life ..synchronised with harmony.. harmonious vibes helping us to feel more alive..the rhythm of life ..feel the beat under your feet ..connect to the mother land..divine feminine..new pathways in your mind..you will feel your one of a kind ..way down deep in your soul ..its time to open the gate ..appreciate..where you've been ..but do come clean ..are you ready ..willing and able ..to open new doors ..step on through..its all waiting for you ..all you've ever dreamed of from your heart and soul ..to come outta the race.. enter the place of grace..and smile ..it will

have been all worthwhile..as you accept your gifts ..to be activated for you to share ..with the world..when your rady ..to share ..you can inspire others ..on there way..and every day remember to smile.. its been a while ..for so many ..as they return home ..to the heart of the matter.. it doesn't matter how long it will take ..just as long as we make the break ..to be free.. sweet liberty..freedom is back ..come out of lack ..set yourself free..

Wonder Through You

SEEING through the wonder of you ..the eyes of a child with innocence ..a new..you will be in awe..of the vibrational wonderland connected to you ..your pure unadulterated consciousness will guide you through in all that you do ..having been released from what was not..true..to then find what was what..this truth sets you free.. surrender into divinity..deep surrender to feel..your energy in motion..emotion.. allow the higher vibrations to keep you afloat ..float on..in the ocean of love ..this unique way to spend your days..gaze awhile be still and smile ..let the waves of love carry you ..surrender to love self worth..self honour..for where you've been and might not have been seen ..for who

you really are ..as the shadows were in the way ..from your sunny disposition.. to express yourself ..so now you know you are sacred in side ..we have a heart and soul combined with our mind ..your whole self will feel more complete..its really neat ..as more senses awaken in your dream within a dream..keep your dream alive ..inside ..hold on to your aspirations ..you will feel your way through in all that you do..let your conscious be your guide ..you will be switched on..to whats going on..take your breath away ..with amazing ..sweet inspirations.. gods spell ..godspeed your love..to ye.. namaste..

Printed and bound by CPI Group (UK) Ltd, Croydon, CR0 4YY